Contents

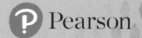

T0352003

Written by
Diana Bentley
Sylvia Karavis
Illustrated by
Peter Richardson

Series editor **Dee Reid**

P Pearson

Characters

Agent Em

Agent Vee

Agent Que

Agent Zed

Chiller

Tricky words

- suddenly
- crackled
- appeared
- everything
- followed
- satellite
- screamed
- vanished

Read these words to the student. Help them with these words when they appear in the text.

Introduction

The four agents were in their Base when suddenly all the alarms went off and an evil face appeared on their screen. It is Chiller, the super-villain, whose ice-ray can turn everything to ice. She plans to freeze everyone to death. Que has a plan but will it stop all the agents dying an icy death?

Chiller

The agents were in the Base when suddenly all the alarms went off.

Then the blank screen crackled into life and an evil face appeared.

"I am Chiller.
My ice-ray turns everything to ice.
Bit by bit I will freeze the world
and everything will die.
If you try to stop me I will freeze you to death."

Then the screen went blank.

"How can we stop her?" said Vee.
Que was thinking hard.

"I have a plan," he said. "We must
wait for Chiller to come here."
"But she will freeze us to death with
her ice-ray," said Em.
"Trust me," said Que. "We must go out
on to the roof."

5

The agents followed Que on to the roof.
They felt an icy chill on their faces.
"Chiller is coming," said Em.

"Get behind the satellite dish," said Que. "Chiller's ice-ray comes from her eyes. If we blind her, she will not be able to freeze us."

Suddenly Vee screamed.
Chiller had appeared and shot her ice-ray at
Vee's foot.

Vee could feel the cold creeping over her foot and up her leg.
Bit by bit she was turning to ice.
She began to slip down the roof.
She could not stop herself.

Quickly Zed pulled
Vee back behind
the satellite dish.
But she was still
turning to ice.

Chiller shot another ice-ray at the agents. But Que grabbed the satellite dish and turned it to face her.

The ice-ray hit the dish.
It shot back at Chiller and
hit her eyes.
Chiller's eyes turned to ice.
"My eyes, my eyes!" she screamed
and then she vanished.

"Good plan," said Em to Que,
"giving Chiller the big freeze!"

"Forget the big freeze, I am turning to ice!" said Vee.
"Chill out!" said Zed. "You can defrost back in the Base!" And the agents carried Vee into the Base.

"Chiller is gone for now," said Que. "But others will try to destroy the world. We must be ready for them."

Quiz ////////////////////////

Text comprehension

Literal comprehension
p4 What was Chiller's plan?
p7 What was Que's plan?

Inferential comprehension
p9 Why was Vee slipping down the roof?
p10 How is Zed brave?
p16 How are the agents feeling at the end?

Personal response
- Do you think Que's plan was good?
- Do you think Chiller might be back?

Word knowledge

p3 Find a word with three syllables.
p11 Which word describes how Chiller speaks?
p13 Find a word that means 'shrieked'.

Spelling challenge

Read these words:

having   next   thing

Now try to spell them!

Ha! Ha! Ha!

What sort of ball doesn't bounce?

A snowball!

Find out about

- Ernest Shackleton and his crew who sailed from England to Antarctica and got trapped in the ice.

Tricky words

- Antarctica
- life-boats
- icy
- Elephant Island
- penguins
- South Georgia
- mountains
- survived

Read these words to the student. Help the with these words wh they appear in the te

Introduction

In 1914 Ernest Shackleton and his crew set out from England to sail to Antarctica. They were going to walk 1,800 miles across the snow and ice. But their ship got trapped in the ice and it sank. When the ice melted, Shackleton had to row off in a life-boat to get help.

Survival

In 1914 Ernest Shackleton and his crew
set out from England to sail to Antarctica.
Then they were going to walk
1,800 miles across the snow and ice.

When the ship got near to Antarctica
the sea began to freeze.
The ship was trapped in the ice.
The ice crushed the ship and it sank.

Shackleton and his men saved the life-boats
and as much food as they could.
For five months they lived on the ice.
Then the ice began to crack.
At last the ice was melting.

They got into the life-boats and set off
across the icy sea.
For a week they rowed hard.
All the men were very cold and hungry.

Then they saw an island.
They knew it was Elephant Island but they
also knew that no-one lived there.

Elephant Island was very cold and icy.
The men used the life-boats as shelters.
They ate seals, penguins and sea birds.

Shackleton knew that no-one would find them on Elephant Island.
If he did not get help soon they would all die.

Argentina

Chile

South Georgia

Elephant Island

South Pole

Antarctic

He took five men and they rowed off
in one of the life-boats.
They rowed for 800 miles.

The sea was very rough
and the men were all very sea-sick.
Many times they thought the boat
would sink.

At last they saw the island of
South Georgia.
They knew people lived there.
They landed but not on the side of the
island where people lived!

Argentina

South Georgia

Elephant Island

South Pole

Antarctic

Shackleton set off with two men
across the icy mountains to get help.
They climbed for 36 hours.
At last they made it to the people of
South Georgia who helped them.

Then Shackleton had to go back to get the men he had left on Elephant Island.

Three times he set off but the sea was too rough. He had to go back.
The fourth time he tried, he made it to Elephant Island and found all his men were alive. At last Shackleton could take them all back to England.

Back in England people said
Shackleton was a hero.
He and his crew had survived
against the odds.

Quiz ////////////////////

Text comprehension

Literal comprehension

p19 Why did Shackleton go to Antarctica?

p30 Why did Shackleton have to go back to Elephant Island?

Inferential comprehension

p21 Why were they glad when the ice began to crack?

p25 Why did Shackleton and the crew have to get away from Elephant Island?

p31 Why did people say Shackleton was a hero?

Personal response

• Would you rather have gone with Shackleton or stayed behind on Elephant Island?

• Do you think Shackleton was a hero? Why?

Word knowledge

p22 Find an adjective which describes the sea.

p25 Find a word that rhymes with 'good'.

p27 Find a word that means the opposite of 'calm'.

Spelling challenge

Read these words:

found   lived   much

Now try to spell them!

Ha! Ha! Ha!

Why don't elephants eat penguins?

Because they can't get the wrappers off!